W0081997

The Mad Farmer's Wife

Poems

By
Rita Sims Quillen

Texas Review Press
Huntsville, Texas

FIRST EDITION
Requests for permission to acknowledge material from the work should be sent to:
> Permissions
> Texas Review Press
> English Department
> Sam Houston State University
> Huntsville, TX 77341-2146

ACKNOWLEDGEMENTS

Poems in this volume appeared previously in the following journals: *Appalachian Heritage, Appalachian Journal, Artemis, Blink, Blue Fifth Review, Connotation Online, The Dead Mule School of Southern Literature, Fried Chicken and Coffee, Georgia Journal, Heartwood, Jimson Weed, Kudzu, Now & Then, Still: The Journal, Town Creek Poetry Review, Pikeville Review, Potomac Review,* and *Texas Review.*
"Prayer of the Mad Farmer's Wife" was an Iron Mountain Press Broadside. "Spring Meditation of the Mad Farmer's Wife" and "Turnips on the Table" appeared in *Something Solid to Anchor To,* a chapbook from Finishing Line Press, 2014. "Chimney Sweep Mother" appeared in *Counting the Sums,* Sow's Ear Press, 1995. "Passing Suite," "Prayer of the Mad Farmer's Wife," and "October Dusk" appeared in *Her Secret Dream,* Wind Press, 2008. "Calving" appeared in the chapbook *October Dusk,* Seven Buffaloes Press, 1987.

Cover art: Angelyn DeBord
Angelyn DeBord has deep roots in the Smoky Mountains of North Carolina which is the source of inspiration for her life as an artist. She is a writer, storyteller, visual artist and registered play therapist. Angelyn continues to live in an isolated area of the Appalachian mountains. She describes her painting style as Appalachian Impressionism. Her work has been collected all over the world. One of her favorite activities in life is hanging clothes out on her big old clothesline and watching them cavort as they whip dry in the sweet mountain air.

adebord@gmail.com
https://www.facebook.com/Art-by-Angelyn-DeBord

Library of Congress Cataloging-in-Publication Data

Names: Quillen, Rita Sims, author.
Title: The mad farmer's wife / Rita Sims Quillen.
Description: Huntsville, Texas : Texas Review Press, [2016]
Identifiers: LCCN 2016015969| ISBN 9781680030990 (pbk. : alk. paper) | ISBN 9781680031003 (e-book)
Subjects: LCSH: Farm life--Poetry. | Women farmers--Poetry. | Appalachian Region--Poetry.
Classification: LCC PS3617.U5356 A6 2016 | DDC 811/.6--dc23 LC record available at https://lccn.loc.gov/2016015969

Dedicated to Wendell Berry
With gratitude and admiration
And to all the
Mad farmers and their wives.

&
For Mac, Teague, and Kelsey

Table of Contents

FOREWORD to THE MAD FARMER'S WIFE

In the early 1980's my husband and I were living on a rocky hillside farm in southwestern Virginia with some cattle, goats, chickens, and two babies while I finished my M.A. at East Tennessee State University in Johnson City, Tennessee. That time in my life is a blur of stress and exhaustion. One thing I remember vividly is discovering the poetry of Kentucky author Wendell Berry. We had studied Berry's essays on farming, the environment, and the economy in my graduate classes, but I was delighted to discover a whole new side of him revealed in his poetry. He had created a brilliant, funny, clear-eyed critic of the modern world called "The Mad Farmer," and the voice in those poems from that persona's perspective was immediately familiar and beloved. Within days of first reading them, I found myself writing a poem from the perspective of the Mad Farmer's Wife—a companion, partner, sounding board, a counterpoint.

As I wrote more poems from her perspective, I realized she was now a permanent character who had taken up residence in my head. Unsure how Mr. Berry would feel about another poet drawing so heavily from his own poetic efforts, I wrote a letter of introduction and enclosed a couple of the poems, asking how he felt about what I was doing and would it be okay if I published some of the poems. He wrote back a very kind and gracious reply, assuring me that he, too, loved the Mad Farmer and was "very glad to finally meet his wife."

Author Ed McClanahan, Berry's long-time friend and neighbor, explains in his introduction to *The Mad Farmer Poems* that we would be mistaken if we misinterpret the character of the Mad Farmer as Berry himself, or even as a spokesperson for him. He is simply one of many characters Berry has assembled over the years for his novels and short stories. Whatever he is, it is clear to me that the Mad Farmer functions effectively as Everyman Farmer of his generation.

The Mad Farmer's Wife and I have a similar relationship. Of course, she speaks out of my head, heart, and experiences. However, in my mind, she is about twelve to fifteen years older than I, has lived a much harder life, has done way more hard labor and farm work, and has seen more change and loss. In short, she's been both luckier and unluckier. She is me and definitely not me.

The Mad Farmer speaks often of his wife, his partner, his love. She is, in fact, central to his life there on the farm, fitting in a most traditional role. Some modern readers may find the Mad Farmer a bit out-of-touch, and he himself says as much in Berry's poem "Some Further Words" when he tells us that he's an "old-fashioned man." As The Mad Farmer goes on to explain in the same poem, modern readers may have no frame of reference for the type of marriage that two people shared on the land in those earlier times, which was both a business partnership and a deep bond of love, trust, and cooperation that is uncommon today. They both fell into very traditional roles on the farm and thought nothing of it. Berry writes:

And just as tenderly to be known
are the affections that make a woman and a man
their household and the homeland one.
These too, though known, cannot be told
to those who do not know them and fewer
of us learn them, year by year
loves that are leaving the world
like the colors of extinct birds
like the songs of a dead language. (34)

The traditional roles and division of labor do not bother the Mad Farmer or his wife. They would be somewhat puzzled to be questioned about gender roles or stereotypes. They go with the flow of nature and time, having no agenda or making no political statement at all beyond a good harvest and doing right by the land, their animals, their neighbors, themselves, their work and their life, doing whatever work there is and, as Berry writes in "The Satisfactions of the Mad Farmer," seeing that it is ". . . done with more than enough knowledge/ and more than enough love/ by those who do not have to be told. (16)"

The Mad Farmer's Wife has a story to tell, some small wisdom she wants to offer the world before she goes, as someone who has lived life at its most elemental level. In these poems she wants us to think about the price of that life, but even more about the price of not living that life. Young women today certainly could teach her a great deal about many things, the practical and the ideological, but they could also learn from her. If nothing else, maybe she can help everyone understand there's only one thing that really matters when it's all said and done and over: love, especially the love between a man and a woman raising a family and working the land together. As the poem "The Mad Farmer Dances" tries to explain, everyone should consider: "The grandest of mysteries — love and its stubbornness — /that wide velvet ribbon holding a marriage/ Made of things so tiny you could breathe them."

Rita Sims Quillen

Berry, Wendell. *The Mad Farmer Poems.* Berkeley: Counterpoint, 2008.

The Mad Farmer's Wife

Traveling Through

A woman walked here once
dozens of tiny bones in her feet crushing delicate growth
breaking leaf spines, crushing them in their flowering.
Their names didn't register,
but it was May Apple
Fern and Buttercups and Periwinkle,
important to somebody here in this sunset.
Careless footfalls as she tries to walk off the pain
of knowing that love isn't enough
shift and scrape and stifle the senses.
October's beauty is a hammer
that will break the lamp with little oil.
Nothing is enough, there is no good enough
to make her leap from limb to limb
like the gray squirrel above.
There is nothing here she can save
even with her pen,
and the loam will someday spring back,
birds will pitch and light
on trees downed in the storms.
You cannot call it healing,
just a scarring.
A woman walked here once.

A Woman Born To Farming

(After Wendell Berry's "A Man Born To Farming")

Skin soft as morning, the mother,
the woman born to farming,
her feet bare on God's green carpet,
gathers apples and pears and eats them.
Her heart is silent, too gentle to beat.
Sometimes it hums or vibrates along a scale,
waits for the call of purpose or need,
while she cans beans, looks for calves, plants seeds.
Sometimes it sends a code
delivered by hummingbird wings.
Her children will call her blessed, the Good Book says,
but mostly they are just too busy to call at all now.
It's not their fault any more
than the leaves that fall from the tree.
They call to her thoughts every day
like the cooing of doves at gloaming,
the whippoorwill reminding us it is dark here.

The farm is a man's world.
She cannot muscle the chainsaw or sick calf,
cannot pick up the heavy hay bales.
Walking in the woods and fields is her job.
Fox bark, turkey putt, buck snort
startle her to answer with laughter.
Words are no help on a farm.
How sad to be good at something unnecessary.
Like the hens and their grit
she has dirt in her craw,
keeps hatching out barren words for others to use.
The Cherokee say Corn Mother
grew corn from her backside,
fed humankind, but the Mad Farmer's Wife
knows it all comes to nothing—
to dark, quiet vastness.
Now it's only the waiting
for the rain, the sun, the next moon change.

Accepting the briers' price,
she gathers raspberries and blackberries,
the stains' temporary tattoo
her only recognition for her work.
She has only the stains
of many things on her empty hands,
the whistled song of days passing in her head.

Prayer Of The Mad Farmer's Wife

May the weeds of August sun grow into heart-shaped hedges
giving symmetry and order to ragged fields.

Let sunburned calves and their tired mothers
find a pool of winter-cool shade.

Between woods and creek at our world's edge
I am lost on a heat-shimmering quilt

just yards from an open door where
my children watch for the relief of nightfall

and aimless bees and flies look to me
saying, "You must know something."

Let there be silence once again
as voices dwindle to snowsoft murmur

My life rising anew from behind the mountain.

Spring Meditation Of
The Mad Farmer's Wife

For Wendell Berry
Ask and it shall be given —
So farming is a laying up
of earthly treasures and fat surprises.
Morels amid brown leaf bed,
brave onions shoving their way into the light,
new pears hanging like joyous tears waiting to fall,
spring gobbler kabuki —
silhouettes in the skyline.
These quests are low stress.
But treks to find calves in late winter —
A different matter all together.
She walks beside, then behind
choosing the path with care
crunching grey and brown stubble
under heavy boots, heavy breathing
bloodrush deafening.
Soon he stops, turns his face
to sun, moon, star
listening for life.
Generations of ancestors
imprinted this imperative: there is no other purpose
here, no meaning, except search and find.
The day is ripening, the rising sun
saffrons the land.
Then he stops, turns to her,
his face breaking into a big grin.
He reaches for her, pulls her close.
The line of grey woods ahead yield
yet another new spring calf
dancing on new legs, sniffing the air.
The Mad Farmer lifts his hand
A blessing and a greeting.

The Chimney Sweep Mother

My baby cannot sleep.
Featherless, red, naked,
streaked with soot,
little chimney sweeps
cry in the blackness
only possible after fire.
Their mother
left them in the fireplace,
the smell of my daughter's crib
drawing her sweet and promiseful.
I carry the quivering nest
to a tree outside,
denying the panic of the mother
who will dive again and again,
swoop and cry into the pitch,
only ancient hopes to guide her search
no light to hide her fear.
Each year
she nests in my daughter's bedroom.
Each year, more cruel than nature,
I carry the nest away.
Mothers never learn:
The wild
trusts and believes in the good
keeps faith
does not surrender.
There will be babies next year.

Canning Ghazal

They are lined up like choir boys, the new treasure:
Sugared suspended peaches look like hearts in my jars.

Hot steam strips the tomatoes of their red dresses.
Blood mush rushes through the funnel to the waiting jar.

Waxy yellow squash and green beans squeak a greeting
bathing beautiful as babies in the new Mason jars.

I need the whole spectrum in dull pantry light,
record of my abundant summer in Technicolor jars.

The lids pop shut on my world and its measure
of love sealed with salty sweat and tears in the perfect jars.

What The Mountains Say

Everyone claims to hear from us
but we've said only "Shhh" forever.
Our tree tongues whisper it
to sun and moon, sun and moon, sun then moon,
way back, long past remembering.
The fog nuzzles with us like an old hound.
The wind screams for our attention.
The creek dances for us like a giddy lover.
The river swallows what we don't want.

Dry bones of dirt farmers like you, piles of them,
rest under brier tangles
roots of maple and oak and poplar.
You deserve better.
It wasn't you who shaved us off like warts
to get at our gems.

You look for God here
but do not see him in our mathematical precision:
Each tree on our face is perfectly formed
 so that the size of the branches
will add up to equal exactly the size of the trunk,
each tree precise and correct.
No guarantee of wisdom or overflowing baskets
to make life fat and full is given,
no pledge to favor your herd,
shade your face but not your garden.
The language of promise was never gifted us.
That's wishful thinking, my friend.
So just bring your sheep
cows, horses, and goats,
bring your boy and girl
your dog and gun.
Bring your boots and matches.
Keep your mind off what's below.

Know the goose skin shivers
of breathing this air.
Rest here and listen to the breeze
move the hairs on your arm.

That is the loudest noise
we'll ever make.

What's Important In
A Graveside Photo — 1898

It isn't the tiny headstone
or those bone-weary ancient eyes in a toddler
standing beside it.
It isn't the barren landscape,
broom sedge and deadly thistles
that smelled like judgment,
or even the wolves I imagine outside the white frame
heads lowered, shoulder bones hefting into their sockets,
in the falling darkness, waiting and watching.

It is the hand
extending from the fur-lined sleeve of the mother
in her finest dress, the hat with a feather.
It is an unfeminine hand — a man hand
that could crush an apple to sauce,
wring off the chicken's head
with one smooth snap of the wrist —
that tries to cover new baby's entire body,

shield it from the camera's eye
saying, "Nothing will get this one."
"Nothing will get this one."

Four Women In Front Of A Sod House

Like proper ladies the three sisters draw our eyes
to their tiny waists, cinched and corseted.
They will ride back to town
where rooms have windows
and boxes for their hats and jewelry,
where tea steeps in pink-flowered china,
but Mabel with her slattern's belly
will stay out here alone
where wind doesn't condemn.
Clouds can't scold.
Her baby will smile up at sun not scorn
out here where a man's last name
carries no weight,
where rich women's pity
won't even dampen the dust.

Another Prayer of the Mad Farmer's Wife

I.

Let me remember this:
Nighttime was always the worst—
long black windows
reflecting back into the room
every single one an abyss.
No streetlights.
No traffic.
No people.
I cried often alone into my pillow
so no one would hear.
One night I stepped off
into the darkness,
let it swallow me
to look back into lighted windows
portals of my life
where my husband and little ones
searched room to room
waited for me
to round the corner
make everything balanced and even
three turned to four.
Another night alone
I retreated upstairs
to bed, desk, lamp, books
under the glaring bulb.
My babies lay in cradling arms
touching my face
while I daydreamed.
We made it to bedtime again.

II.

Let me find my path:
On the farm I could walk.
Two barns to visit—
one up on the hill
had a loft with a view of a pudding bowl field
of cedars, wild roses, rotting fence.
Down at the creek a clear pool
reflected the daylight.
Another place to walk
was the high ridge cliff
where I could hang
in the skyline over the river.
At the edge of life
was the garden,
wet, ripe, and ragged
with perfect rows
of lush symmetry.
In town I walk narrow streets,
step off sidewalk blocks—
a bone train on a slab track—
feeling no release.
No one can think and walk
in this concrete maze.
There is danger from streets,
strangers who stop and stare—
the clippers of hedges
mowers of lawns
tenders of roses.
I come home after going nowhere.

III.

Let me be heard:
We don't sell our souls
or just lose them
the way men sometimes do.
We usually give them away.
How did our mothers manage?
My mother never ran out
into the night
paced ridges like a wolf,
stood alone in darkness
under a canopy of stars,
but she did cry into her pillow:
I remember that.
Even as a child
I knew to listen,
to feel that sound and know it
as a sign.

The Mad Farmer's Wife Delivers the Foal

It is the turning I most remember:
Just another ordinary day.
I woke and looked out the window.
The mare stood with the colt half out of her,
membrane still completely intact.
I ran like a warrior, butcher knife in hand,
stabbed into that death bubble,
liquid gushing out, the foal lifeless.
I had sense enough to wonder for a moment
Will she kick me?
But she just looked back.
It is the turning I still remember
wide-eyed, nostrils flaring
while we shared the stare of horror.
I grabbed the one front leg,
pulled and pulled and we both fell.
Rain began beating down.
Her body heaved and squeezed
her baby, its lifeless tongue lolled out.
As I lay on my back on the ground for the first time
in a long, long time, with raindrops falling on my face,
I pulled and pulled once more and in a rush
like an earthquake or a heartbreak
the motionless gorgeous dappled foal was free
of her, of me, of the fence and rain, of earth.
I opened my mouth to the sky's tears.
We all lay there in that stunned moment,
both the living panting, me crying.
It is the turning I remember
She only raised her head again, stared
at what could never be,
then looked away
out across the dark cedar thicket and pine shadows
while I dragged myself to my feet
to stagger up to the house and coffee and shower.
I got ready and went on to work
Death School having let out early.

Coyote Lament

O bleak blind mindless death,
you come in silence:
The roar of the wind takes my breath.
Even if I had a gun
I could not kill you at such distance.
but the calves will not realize at all
until you are very near,
and their hysterical mothers
driven by a knowledge carried like a curse
will paw and throw their heads in anguish.
In a world of instantaneous communication,
laser surgery, and space travel,
you come from the cave of history
to destroy at will, unafraid and unfettered.
Oh dog-cousin, wolf-brother,
what onyx lesson do you bring us
but to see that beauty can be evil
and evil can be beauty,
that blood sacrifices are still required,
that tenders and keepers are neither:
Merely watchers.

The Grey Fox

I couldn't believe it
when I saw him—
flashing beauty against the blinding snow
limping along the fence inside the yard,
the artificial boundary between
the world and the wild.
Carrying one leg, he owed
no explanation for the breach.
Just beyond the fence at the woods' edge,
regal and ramrod straight,
he sat down and stared intently
at me through the window
already a ghost,
my memory his only heir
before coyotes delivered his fate.
What an honor to be sought
by what's broken,
to be called to testify
for one on trial for his life.

Cemetery

Every home should have its own cemetery
like we have on our farm.
It's a fenced-in garden of worn white stones,
some tiny, for the little ones taken by fever,
some large and ornate, for those who survived childhood.
Even on our happiest days
when laughter rings like a March wind
it is in the back of our minds, the edge of vision:
where we're headed.
I've never gone inside the graveyard fence,
never touched the tombstones a century old,
but I've stared long at the tiny ones,
eaten the dank mossy air
that rolls out of the sentinel hemlocks standing watch.
I cannot think anything except they were happy,
cannot bear to dream that they felt empty
and wondered why, or worse, knew.

Calving

In agony the cow wandered in circles.
The Mad Farmer waited.
March rain dripped
steady annoying wetness
that made the pain worse.
Cow charged, rage and steam rising
from her bloated body,
her eyes glazed and hard:
She thought he caused the pain.
In the barn later
he roped her to a rafter,
tied her off to her pain.
She had to get on with it.
They struggled together
through the night,
the heavy dark like a hand around the throat.
Finally, he felt his way to the calf,
pulled it choking but well
from the prison of bone,
all three covered with blood
water and earth.

Weariness lifted by relief,
carried away by the dawn mist.
The Mad Farmer untied the cow
then did a quick sidestep like Fred Astaire
when she tried her best to kill him.
He laughed and whistled out of the barn,
went home to eat his breakfast,
the sun plowing the morning sky.

The Mad Farmer's Wife Throws A Cuss Fit

She wasn't raised that way.
Occasionally her mom would let fly
when long days with four little heathens
wore down the filter.
Still, ladies weren't supposed to act like that.
Marriage brought her a man, however,
who considered cussing an art,
a masculine craft worthy of cultivation.
> He could cuss the bark off a hickory
> A calf through the fence
> A bent bolt back through a bracket
> A frozen lug wrench off a tractor tire rim.
Always a good student,
she apprenticed for years
before her skills matured.
It was a frozen water line
exploding in the kitchen,
water ankle-deep on new linoleum,
him gone, her pregnant to bursting
having to crawl under the house
in her nightgown in Arctic wind:
This was her moment.
She was speaking in tongues
but no glossolalia here:
Every word crisp, clear and precise,
an epic conflagration of every verbal horror
she could muster,
every bite of that forbidden fruit
spit back at the world.
> But he still had to use a blowtorch
> To finally thaw the line when he got home.
> One can't really expect transfiguration
> Right out of the gate.

A Poet's Vegetable Epiphany

Gardens are a perpetual gift.
I don't mean all the tomatoes and cucumbers,
sweet snap peas multiplying in piles.
I'm talking metaphor—
Their symmetrical shapes, every color and smell
whimsical overgrown lushness and sensuality,
an artist's dream.
You can talk about laying out perfect rows—
the spacing, the preparation, the tending—
about harvest and pestilence,
storms and scavengers, about plants
that look gorgeous
but never mature—
about earthly treasure and heaven's promise,
roots and buds
as if the garden was created by a poet,
someone who knew
we needed things to gather and eat,
the juice dripping off our pens.

When the Children Come Home

When the children come home
we don't kill the fatted calf,
but we do cook both ham and turkey,
casseroles and pies and fruit,
table groaning under the sacrament
borne of blood and absence,
every visit prodigal in its intensity
but not really:
Because they aren't staying.

When the children come home
and then leave again,
we look at the acres cleared inch by inch,
dollar by dollar,
the fence built foot by sweaty, bleeding foot
wonder why in the world
why
in the world we have spent
the one tiny spark from a campfire
that is our time here
on giving them something they need
like a rotary telephone or a wringer washer.
Imagine strangers wandering through
Saying, "How much?"
our fields taken back by wild rose
bull thistle,
the auctioneer's gavel
sounding a death knell.
Words of such love,
such longing choke in our throats
a cry or a sigh
never told until that final day
after all is said and done and over
when the children come home.

Just Fishing

The fact it's a cliché
doesn't interfere with its beauty or truth:
The three men are a ballet
in front of a green curtain.
One leans into the cast,
line arcing just under the canopy
while another crouches to collect
the slice of silver quivering in his net.
The third, the oldest, moves slow,
deliberate and stylized like a kabuki dancer,
pausing on each stone
testing its resting place:
Testament to why he's lived so long.
Water music and wind rush,
bird songs and wing rhythms
 ring and echo off sheer rock ledge —
a symphony worthy of this place.
The best part is the absence of words.
It is creek grace.

There will be plenty of time for silence
when the long sleep comes
but we'll be ignorant of it.
Here and now we can stick our hand
in this swift cold current,
our tongue to the cup,
ear to the wind,
crawl inside our head and shut the door.
Isn't it strange how we cast for words
our whole lives,
do the slow dance
before the white curtain of paper,
catch them in our net
then feel the joy and peace of release,
knowing full well the only honest prayer
that anyone can pray
is the one without words?
The fact that it's cliché
doesn't interfere with its beauty or truth.

What Birds Say

(For William Stafford)

What birds say, that is what I say, too.
Redbirds dangle like Christmas balls in pines
reminding us of winter's sweet silence.
Their wings whisper "Blood" as they sail by:
How fragile the unseen bond
clotting everything together.

Hummingbirds use sign language
To give instruction:
So much for gravity and physics and expectations.
We are God's calling card.
Just follow us right back to Him.

Bluebirds straddle the birdhouse rooftop
shout "Again" as they fly a thousand sorties
gathering and feeding and gathering more.
Watch them and forget everything
that is not blue.

Whippoorwills preach persistence
the power of the frantic
the beauty of the trill—
that we must always, always
sing ourselves into the dark.

The Hawk lords over us all—
barks orders to surrender
kills the weak.
Some say the word "Majestic" up at him
but I do not.
I never speak to spirits.

Only after they are gone
I whisper one word:
What the birds say, that is what I say, too.

I Woke Up Late

I woke up late and missed everything—
The news and weather and breakfast and a poem,
stumbled to the coffee pot and front windows
to see if the ridgeline could tell me what day it was.
It rises and falls like a heartbeat across the pasture.
Next thing I know, I have my clothes and boots
walking fast, faster toward the deep woods
down the steep rocky way
to the whirling eddy in the creek.
I wish I could jump in it and be carried backwards
spit out on another shore
where my children are still small
and I give them fish I caught and my thoughts,
where they are owls with divine eyesight
miraculous beyond the telling.
Next thing I know there's this baby
With smiles so sweet its imagining floods my eyes.
He will not remember me or my way,
even if I catch the fish and feed it to him,
if my thoughts become the owl
and sit on his gloved hand,
if my heart becomes the beating ridge steadying the sky.
I woke up late and missed everything.

He Tells Her A Love Poem

This is all your fault—
every bit of it.
When we came here for the first time,
you said, "I want my house right there,"
like I could wave my hand
turn bull thistle, broom sedge,
Joe-pye and Goldenrod into
Orchardgrass and flowers,
turn a wilderness into a retreat,
a little beaten path into a doorway.
Well, no use whining:
So I set to doing it.
A house, barn, ponds,
sheds, gates, wells dug,
eight miles of fence,
cedars cut and piled to the sky
buckets of sweat later,
fifteen years of it,
and I still look over at you
sitting on the porch
smiling at the ridgeline,
your pretty hands cradling your cup,
and the rush of feeling
fills my eyes, catches in my throat.
I can read all kinds of sign—
know the smell of weather
the ways of everything living
but you are the mystery
I can't solve.
You are the why
in every sore muscle and bloody blister
the root of every tangle
every strike of the ax
every shovel full of dirt
turned in search of the key
to your heart's puzzle.

She Answers With A Love Poem
Of Her Own

I was going to write a love song
but wrote about two Bluebirds instead.
Their love is never going to go wrong.
They'll stick together and keep their babies fed.

I tried again to write a love song,
wrote about two Redbirds instead.
Their love rides along on wings so strong
they have no words, nothing need be said.

I'm finally going to write a love song
not write about the Blackbirds instead.
Years and years go by and our love rolls on.
We face the future together without dread:

We fret and doubt
light on different trees.
Our souls don't need hands to hold,
just wings touching wings on a breeze.

Come

Let me whistle this to you, this love song,
my pursed lips inches from your neck
sweet breath warmed
as it passes through my heart,
lifting the song
to Meadowlark, Wren, and Thrush,
all the colors of love
floating overhead.

What the Creek Says

You look to the clouds
to the blue blankness overhead,
cross yourselves, fall to your knees
talk sharp shards of stars
brittle black emptiness.
No, look down at your toes in the silt:
God says "Good morning."
His creatures waste no time looking up.
The rippling speech of the creek,
rhythmic grinding of the foraging cows,
heads all bowed to their green communion,
are the liturgy and homily of this, the richest cathedral.
When everything else has changed, even the heavens,
I have not. I will stay water, no matter what comes.
There is a reason I am ritual,
every kind of metaphor,
the only balm for every kind of sore.

Heritage Apples

I need to talk about apples.
City folk only know the famous ones:
Red and Golden Delicious and Winesap
Gala and Granny Smith.
A few who remember the smell of woodsmoke might name
Summer Rambo or Juneapple.
Just as with most things,
what is popular is the least substantive.
The apple has been simplified, smoothed-out
commercialized from the untamed perfection of creation.
They mutated and crossed and were reborn
in every conceivable combination of traits.
Purists study and propogate them,
attempt to bring the obscure treasures
back into our hands,
calling them "heritage apples."
There are books devoted to cataloging them
adding to the list of hundreds and hundreds of kinds.
Their names lilt across the breeze
Cox Orange Pippin and Virginia Beauty
Arkansas Black and Mountain Boomer
Roman and Ruby Red and Sunday Sweet.
No other food comes in so many varieties.
Why are there so many kinds of apples?
Corn and beans and potatoes have no such abundance.
Could it be that the story of The Fall,
the saddest of family stories,
points to the answer:
For such a sweet and lovely thing
as an apple to wear that burden
of symbol of sin,
it must become every kind imaginable.

What the Rock Says

I've been waiting for you.
My only virtue is patience.
I am something different
from what I was,
but you can no more see me
than yourself.
Aren't you always shocked
at your reflection?
You have hands, feet, a mouth
but are no more useful than me.
I laugh at the poet
who imagines the cosmos inside me,
imagines maps to stars,
heiroglyphics from heaven
etched by the unseen hand.
I have no eyes at all
but see more than you.
I have seen the Kingsnake
wind up a branch
slow as dawn,
eat the nesting Bluebird's babies
in horrific silence,
watched the hawk drop from the clouds
to snag the rabbit from its sleepy browsing,
saw two bucks fight, heads high in the air,
horns locked in a war for ground.
The only time you notice me
is when I turn your ankle
or bear your name.

Passing Suite

(For Ann Richman)

I.

Among all the things
she wished for at the end:
Two white shirts,
her book of Shakespearean sonnets
and the sound of his steady breathing
napping in the chair at her bedside.
She dreamed snap peas and raspberry vinaigrette
tall Dahlias, Snapdragons, Nasturtium,
yellow-fringed Orchids
she hiked three miles to see,
spoke soft vowels
carrying Carolina Wrens
Eastern Bluebirds
Ruby-throated Hummingbirds
the white crane
that took out her father's eye.

II.

There's aesthetically appealing Death:
The face of a dying foal
I have just liberated
from leathery placenta with a butcher knife,
the performance art of a Kingsnake
majestically digesting
the whole nest of baby Bluebirds
framed in the perfect background
of azure sky and emerald hill.
But the real inheritance of Mother Nature:
A skeleton with skin
gasping loudly for air,
lungs filled with cancer's froth,
the air heavy with a sister's wailing.

III.

I am resigned
to a thickening waist
deeply lined skin,
surprised in my mirror
by my wrinkly smile.

Wild gray hairs
sprout like little exclamation marks
all around my face
fitting punctuation
for little daily epiphanies.

I relax into a soft pillow of years.
The body fades
so sense and spirit can flourish—
Middle age is molting season.

IV.

My children are strong
beautiful, confident, defiant
but plain blind ignorant—
life has not paid them a visit yet.

When they were home
they put up posters,
collages of images from magazines
where they could be Creator
God.

My daughter called today
to say she was moving to New Jersey
so she wouldn't grow up
to be me.
(She didn't actually say that last part.)
In New Jersey they aren't pathetic
provincials: they know wine and design
and nineteenth-century Parisian art.

Up there things move so fast
Death can't even blow a cold breath
in a room, let alone grab hold of you.
There's no silence to be found
so she's safe.

V.

Will they say I made a good end?
Even if I don't, I think
I'll copy her—
ask for the shirts and sonnets
in case the Bible and fiddle music aren't enough,
pray for grace and peace,
for once in my life
try to go natural, right, and quiet
as a summer storm passing.

Turnips on the Table

How odd when a vegetable and person merge
becoming one in your mind and mouth.
My grandmother loved those little roots.
Their stealthy sting hit your tongue
like an angry truth.
Put all the butter and sugar you want—
their heat cannot be denied.
No wonder they're shaped like tears.

They owned a little grocery store,
could eat anything they wanted
but hardscrabble childhood hangs on you,
a bell that can't be unrung.
Turnips on the table:
A reminder of a hard battle won,
a daily bitter tear on the tongue.

Love Lesson

What I know about love
I learned from you whose hands
mapped all my imperfect geography,
tamed dangerous undercurrents
and left a fingerprint of scent—
an address of desire.

The Mad Farmer Dances

The Mad Farmer is no leading man,
No cowboy or warrior.
She is nothing special —
simply his axis, the equator
of the world that is the farm.
He loves to catch her rising from her bath
the same as the hawk rising from the poplar,
watches her work in garden or kitchen
slantwise, so she won't notice him.
Who needs art
when nature is at your hip, at your fingertip?
The grandest of mysteries — love and its stubbornness —
that wide velvet ribbon holding a marriage
made of things so tiny you could breathe them.
He would die for her without a moment's hesitation.
It makes her weep to think of it
but that is not the same as saying she's happy.
No, what holds her is memory
that blows by
like starlings in the summer's quiet,
quick and brief but color so vivid:
It was a soft night —
Ernest Tubb's Midnight Jamboree
played Loretta Lynn singing "Until I Met You."
He pulled her from the kitchen
to the darkened front room and the fire,
held her close, firm, as if she might pull away,
danced, holding her hand high in the air.
Across the floor they minced,
eyes closed like some silly movie,
warm skin and breath and smell
of laundry and soap and supper.
The velvet ribbon is tied in a big bow
around their world.
Young ones are blind to it,
the why and how, invisible,
as are the starling and hawk
the dance and the ribbon.

October Dusk

(For Mac)

The evening dark
falls all around me,
its warm breath
casts a shadow on my face.

Sitting on my front steps,
I am a candle flame
drawing moths and mosquitoes
holding the moments in my cupped hands.

He sits quietly by me
memories of the day's work
swift moving color shared
like fall leaves in the yard.

The potatoes from the garden
lie scattered in the grass.
Tomorrow we will sort them
and store them for winter.

His hand rests on my neck
as he slowly stands.
He offers the other dirty hand
to help me up.

Our eyes meet in the fading light.
We go inside
surrendering to night—
the smell of earth still strong.